The Two of Us

Reflections on Shared Growth in Marriage

Herb & Mary Montgomery

Winston Press

Acknowledgments

Listed in order of appearance:
Gift from the Sea by Anne Morrow Lindbergh, Random House
The Art of Loving by Erich Fromm, Harper & Row
Between Man and Woman by Everett Shostrom and James Kavanaugh,
    Nash Publishing
I'm OK—You're OK by Thomas A. Harris, M.D., Harper & Row
A Baby?...Maybe by Dr. Elizabeth M. Whelan, Bobbs-Merrill
Marriage Is the First Step toward Divorce by Pamela Mason with Vi Wolfson,
    Paul S. Ericksson
Conceptions of Modern Psychiatry by Harry Stack Sullivan, W. W. Norton
Open Marriage by Nena O'Neill and George O'Neill, M. Evans
Love, Liberation, and Marriage by Dorothy T. Samuel, Funk & Wagnalls
To Understand Each Other by Paul Tournier, John Knox Press
Joyce Carol Oates quote from "The Good Life on Earth"
    in *McCall's,* January 1970
Loving Free by Paula and Dick McDonald, Grosset & Dunlap
Marriage for Beginners by Mary Williams, Macmillan
The Intimate Marriage by Howard J. Clinebell, Jr., and Charlotte H. Clinebell,
    Harper & Row
The Brothers System for Liberated Love and Marriage by Dr. Joyce Brothers,
    Peter H. Wyden

Photographs by
Camerique: 7, 8, 17, 19, 27, 33, 36, 39, 41,
    43, 44, 52, 55, 59, 61, 63, 64
Alan Cliburn: 28
Kay Freeman: 20
Olof Källström: 15
Freda Leinwand: 51
Jean-Claude Lejeune: 5, 48
Robert Maust: 12
Diana Palting: 23
Rick Smolan: 35, 47, 56
Bob Taylor: 31
Vivienne: 11, 24

Winston Press, 430 Oak Grove, Minneapolis, MN 55403

Contents

The Beginning

Marriage is an opportunity to satisfy the yearning we all feel for meaningful closeness with another person. It's a chance to give love, and in doing so, we hope to receive it. But to make what attracted us to the person we married grow into something deep and enduring takes time, patience, and the will to make it happen.

Most of us have an image of what marriage should be that derives from the times in which we live. In today's world, there are many marriage patterns from which to choose. Married people may or may not have children. Both partners may work away from home or they may take turns holding jobs. One may always work away from home while the other elects to be the homemaker. Men can be househusbands just as women can be housewives. It is up to each couple to decide which marriage style best enables both partners to grow to their full capacity as persons.

In every marriage there are arid times when the partners feel their needs are not being met, times when it may even appear easier to end the relationship than to work out its problems. That's when we need to retain faith in our commitment, reconsider those areas in which we agree, and recall qualities we like about one another. Frequently, we'll find more good things in our marriage than we thought there were.

As the authors of *The Two of Us,* we stress the belief that a man and woman in love can work out a marriage style that enables them to grow both as individuals and as a couple. Together they can share experiences of growth that single people often struggle through alone. In the process each can become stronger and wiser.

Many factors influence marriage today, but in the end, it is the "two of us" — couple by couple — who determine what life together will be. Making the most of marriage means making the most of ourselves as people. When we help one another do that, we come to a new understanding of the promise of love that we made on our wedding day.

Mary Montgomery
Herb Montgomery

Cutting Through the Marriage Myths

We grow up with the romantic idea that love overcomes all obstacles and enables us to live happily ever after in marriage. Surely *it is possible* to create a happy and lasting marriage, but doing so requires the use of the head as well as the heart.

Early in marriage, when the heart is passionately in charge, we're likely to believe the romantic myths of our society. The sooner we recognize and go beyond these myths, the sooner we'll begin sharing the genuine richness of living as couples. The most common myths include beliefs like the following:

We marry because of love.

Marriage cures loneliness.

Marriage completes us as a person.

Marriage, a home, and a child will make us happy.

There's only one person in the world for each of us.

Experts tell us that, although we say we marry for love, we're really marrying for other reasons. It may be our fear of living alone, our sex drive, a need for approval, or a desire to improve ourselves. Of course, love and marriage do go together, but the depth of love is revealed only through time, as we mature and give up our self-centeredness. By itself, marriage won't cure our loneliness or add a missing half to complete us as persons, but a satisfying relationship can help us grow in self-understanding and become more secure. Marriage, a home, and a child are externals. They do not create permanent happiness. Happiness, in the long run, must develop from within as the result of becoming a real and loving person. Surely it is good to feel that we *belong with* our mate, but as we come to understand love, we give up the selfish thought that there's just one person created for each of us.

Cutting through the myths may upset our dreams of happiness and fulfillment, but that's not the purpose for doing so. Our reason for looking beyond myths is to find the solid ground on which to create a satisfying married life. That ground is the understanding that marriage is a deeply complex human relationship. It involves us in giving, tending, caring, sharing, and finally opening ourselves to the wonder of love.

Security in a relationship lies neither in looking
back to what it was in nostalgia, nor forward
to what it might be in dread or anticipation, but
living in the present relationship and accepting it
as it is now.

Anne Morrow Lindbergh

Making
the
Commitment

At some point in our relationship, we may have the blissful feeling that our love can't be improved upon and shouldn't ever change. We say such things as "Stay just the way you are!" This is like telling the flowering fruit tree to remain at the blossoming stage instead of growing through the seasons. In a relationship, as in the rest of nature, the cycle of seasons is one of change. Within every successful marriage, there is one thing that enables a couple to change through the years and still grow in love. That is the commitment each person feels.

There are reasoned commitments and there are emotional commitments. A reasoned one is like a legal contract that is a fixed promise we are obligated to meet. An emotional commitment is given freely out of love. After meeting a person, most of us go through a series of steps. Meeting leads to knowing and knowing leads to liking and liking leads to loving. At some point in the relationship, a feeling of emotional commitment makes itself known within us.

Although emotional commitment is a crucial—and natural—part of a happy marriage, it is not a promise or an obligation. Rather, it is a way of living together that involves the unfolding and revealing of ourselves. It is something we do because we want to, not because we have to.

Instead of being firmly and for all time emotionally committed, we are always *becoming* committed. This is an active process with a flow of caring created by mutual respect and concern. We give and receive, receive and give.

When there is emotional commitment, our trust grows. Then, we are able to drop pretending and pretense. As the mask of self-protection slips away, we find ourselves open to becoming the good and human person each of us was created to be. Unlike a reasoned obligation, which tends to divide responsibilities into "yours and mine," our developing emotional commitment unites "you" and "me" as "us." It enables us to establish a comfortable flow of giving and receiving that increases the love in marriage.

To love means to commit oneself without guarantee, to give oneself completely in the hope that our love will produce love in the loved person. Love is an act of faith. . . .

Erich Fromm

Being Friends with One Another

At its very best, marriage is a friendship between two people who really like each other. As newlyweds, we're apt to be so consumed by romantic feelings that friendship gets overlooked. Hopefully, as the anniversaries come and go, romance will remain a dynamic force in our relationship and we'll also discover that the person we married is our friend as well as our lover.

Becoming a friend with our mate — even a best friend — is a possibility at any time. Many people for whom marriage followed "love at first sight" find that becoming friends later is an unexpected bonus. Others who married someone who was already a close friend find romance growing with time. In both instances, being friends increases the joy of marriage.

A key to building friendship is the use of time for pursuits that please both partners. Whatever we enjoyed together before the wedding we'll probably continue to enjoy afterwards. Sharing interests — whether it's skiing, collecting antiques, or tossing a frisbee — fosters friendship. Of course, as time passes, our interests and needs change, leading us to seek new activities. Some activities may create a spirit of competitiveness between us. By keeping it on a friendly level, we'll find that whatever we do together gives us enjoyment and much to talk about.

Sharing fully with the person we married is good, but not to the point of possessiveness. Friends want what is best for each other. Friendship in marriage includes trust and the freedom to grow as separate individuals.

After marriage, it's wise to retain old friendships and nurture new ones as well. With these individual friends, we may broaden our knowledge and pursue interests that have limited appeal to our mate. As long as our commitment to each other comes first, outside friends are likely to strengthen a good marriage.

The more sensitive we are to each other's needs and the more we respect one another's separate identities, the freer we are to grow in love and in friendship. What a good feeling it is when one day we realize that the person we've married is our very best friend!

It is individuals, capable of loving and being loved, who can truly build a marriage. Their marriage will not absorb their individuality, nor destroy their individual goals, nor push them into artificial roles. They will know that only by being themselves can they relate to each other.

Everett Shostrom and James Kavanaugh

Knowing Our Goals

Married life can be as smooth as a ride on a bicycle built for two or as rough as a tug-of-war. It depends largely on whether we're facing the same direction and coordinating efforts or opposing one another by pulling from opposite sides. Our chance of developing a rewarding marriage increases when we share both short and long-range goals.

Short-range goals involve everyday things such as meeting the monthly bills, planning a party, or taking a weekend trip. Sharing and working on these goals helps us live smoothly through a day, a week, and a month at a time. Long-range goals involve such things as getting more education, having a child, buying a home, and moving to another part of the country. We may agonize over setting and reaching such goals for months or even years.

The dreams and specific goals that we consider important will conflict sometimes with our mate's ideas. One may want to vacation in the mountains while the other prefers the beach. One may want a house while the other is set on apartment living. Does one simply give in and then live forever with a crippled dream? No, that's neither smart nor fair. Instead, we must discuss our goals on a regular basis, modify them to meet reality, and take specific actions toward reaching those we agree on.

The more specific we make our goals, the easier it is for our partner to respond creatively. The desire to be happy is too vague a goal. We need to pin the idea of happiness to something concrete. For example, one's goal may be to own a motel. When one partner shares this dream, the other could respond creatively by pointing out that although there's little money saved for a down payment, going to work for a motel chain would be a way to gain business experience while continuing to save. That would add reality to the idea without crippling the dream.

Love bonds us together with another person as a couple and makes it unfair for either to pressure the other into accepting what that person doesn't believe in. Flexibility and open-mindedness help us remain close as we talk about our differences and modify our goals. Then by committing ourselves to a plan of action, we can indeed make dreams come true.

Decisions regarding hobbies, possessions,
where to live, and what to buy must be made
according to a set of values and realistic
considerations unique to the marriage.

Thomas A. Harris, M.D.

Deciding about Parenthood

Although "the two of us" are already a family, sooner or later we'll feel pressured to make up our minds about having children. Arguments for and against parenthood come from our parents and in-laws, the church, and a society that, in general, favors having children.

In making up our mind about parenthood, it's important to ask basic questions such as:

Are we both aware that raising a child involves at least eighteen years of our life?

Do we know one another well enough, or might the stress of a child be a divisive force?

Would a baby create a conflict over careers?

Will we be able to financially support a child?

Is our reason for having a baby purely selfish? (That is, is it based on the egotism of creating life or of carrying on the family name?)

Are both partners prepared to give time and energy to loving a third person who might not be completely normal?

We all approach the questions about parenthood as beginners with a lot to learn. So the more we understand ourselves as individuals and as a couple, the more likely we are to make a decision that we'll be comfortable living with. Not all of us should have children. There is nothing wrong with admitting this, choosing a child-free life, and living without guilt or apology!

If we enter marriage with a baby already on the way, our union is a bit more likely to end in dissolution than if we wait longer to have a child. Knowing this, we need to work even harder at developing a supportive relationship with our mate. Whenever a child arrives, it can strain a marriage, but with mutual understanding we can overcome the stress and create a happy life.

Whether or not to be a parent is a very emotional issue. Outsiders give well-meant advice, but the final decision remains with us as a couple. Whether we choose to be child-free or to create a new life, it's a decision that we make together. In the process of deciding, let the words between us be quiet ones of love, for it's nobody's business but our own.

Know who you are singly and who you are as a couple. Know...what your strengths and your weaknesses are, what you have to offer, and what a child would simply have to tolerate. Self-awareness is the best, most reliable way to reach the final decision about whether or not you would like to be a parent.

Dr. Elizabeth M. Whelan

Sharing the Load

Fairness must be a guiding principle as we establish a living pattern in marriage. But in sharing the load, more is involved than merely a fair division of the work. Two people should also share in respecting, comforting, and freeing one another to grow as equals.

Those of us who come from families where sharing was determined by tradition may feel it's a woman's duty to cook, clean, and care for children. Also, we might consider it a man's obligation to earn the money and to maintain the house and car. This family pattern, which developed long ago, is only one way for a couple to divide the major tasks. Since life today is very different than it was a generation ago, feelings of being unduly burdened or trapped by marriage may develop if we accept such a style of living without question.

Through sharing, it's possible to avoid such problems. Teaching each other the living skills we have acquired individually makes us more resourceful. A man who can sort, wash, dry, fold, and put away laundry is an informed and capable partner who is more apt to appreciate and respect the necessity of this work. The same is true of a woman who knows how to check the car's battery, tires, radiator, oil, and automatic transmission fluid. Through such skill-sharing we rid ourselves of fixed notions we may have about women's and men's roles, and we add to our self-esteem.

But no matter how confident we may be, there are times when we feel psychological burdens. Pressures to have a child, maintain a social life, pay off bills, or advance in a career can lead to unbearable weariness if we must carry them alone. As comforters we can share such pressures through conversation with our mate and then plan ways to alleviate the stresses. Even the worst problems seem less burdensome when we know someone else understands *and* cares.

One of the benefits of being married is having someone with whom to share. Sharing makes us open and honest and helps us achieve personal growth. We know we're partners in a life of love when each of us can look back at the end of a day and feel a genuine sense of dignity and pride because of what we have done both alone and together.

To make a long-time life-long marriage there
must be an enormous amount of mutual
understanding, mutual consideration and mutual
dreams plus a willingness to meet in the middle.

Pamela Mason with Vi Wolfson

Handling the Money

Attitudes toward money are formed early in childhood. Did our parents pay bills on time, or were anxious creditors an accepted part of life? Was money saved on a regular basis or spent with abandon? Whether or not we recognize it, we bring some of our parents' money habits to our own marriage. Quite naturally if "your" money and "my" money become "our" money, the potential for conflict is great. It is so great that many counselors rate disagreements over money as the leading cause of divorce. The problem may arise over the amount of money a couple has, but more often it develops over failure to agree on spending.

For each of us money has different meanings, so we need to share what it represents to us. To one, it may mean security or status. To the other, it might be independence or achievement. It means power to virtually all of us. Once we've discussed the significance we attach to money, it's no longer a mystery why one prefers a boat to new carpeting or a luxury car to a compact model. Understanding our attitudes opens the door to making agreements about spending that are mutually acceptable.

Every couple needs some method of money management. The simplest one is to determine first the income and expenses for such fixed items as housing, food, transportation, and utilities. Both partners should know how to pay the bills and balance the checkbook, but the jobs are best done by the one who is more willing and more qualified. We lessen many tensions that arise over finances by discussing questions such as: "Which serves us better, joint or separate accounts? How can we improve our credit rating? Should we be saving more or less?"

What's left after the bills are paid can be a cause for dispute or a source of great satisfaction. To make it the latter, every couple needs an agreed-upon plan for the use of any extra money. It might mean having a big night out or adding to savings for a special purchase. What the extra money is spent for doesn't matter as long as it really is "extra" and the needs of both partners are taken into consideration. A most helpful guideline is to use whatever money remains after the basic expenses are covered to enrich our life and our marriage.

When the satisfaction or the security of another
person becomes as significant to one as is
one's own satisfaction or security, then
the state of love exists.

Harry Stack Sullivan

Facing Annoyances

As creatures of habit, each of us has peculiarities of which we are unaware and with which we are comfortable. Living in intimate closeness with another person alerts us to our differing habits. One of us may be neat and the other sloppy—one of us punctual and the other always late.

The bathroom has a way of revealing more minor annoyances and petty irritations than practically any other place. There's a ring of shaved stubble left around the sink or tub. There's something soaking in the sink when we want to wash our hands. There's an empty roll of toilet tissue on the holder, and the toothpaste tube is mashed in the middle.

These examples are the stuff out of which conflict is created. Petty annoyances? Indeed. And any one of them might be simply and easily corrected. But if we say nothing about the other's peculiarities and the displeasure they create, the irksome actions will build up within us like a volatile gas just waiting to be ignited. When the spark comes—and it's usually from something unrelated to the irritation—the explosion is very loud and very real!

How *do* we handle such exasperating quirks?

First of all, it's important to realize that, whether it's knuckle cracking or the way our mate parks a car that irritates us, the habit is only one small part of the total person. And we love that person! Communication then becomes the only way to resolve the irritation. The objective is to share, in a direct but kind way, a request for a minor change of behavior. Having a sense of humor helps; so does the ability to encourage the other person to see that some benefit will come with change. For example, if it's a messy bathroom sink that upsets us, we might say, "A dirty sink really irritates me. I'd be in a better mood if you'd clean up after yourself." Admitting our annoyances in a non-threatening way sets the scene for change and long-lasting compatibility.

True intimacy between mates, and mutual
growth, is based on the ability to open up
and share your inner selves without fear of
judgment — not only your likes, but your dislikes,
your doubts as well as your hopes.

Nena O'Neill and George O'Neill

Fighting Constructively

Two people sharing their lives in the constant and intimate relationship of marriage are sure to face occasional friction. Situations arise that cause anger, resentment, jealousy. To maintain harmony we may be tempted to suppress what we feel, but doing so will only put up a barrier. This barrier will become higher if we continue to ignore problems and deny feelings.

A confrontation may be painful, but in the end it will add to the health of marriage. Facing disagreements serves as an emotional house-cleaning that leads to greater trust and understanding. By following a few ground rules, a confrontation can be a constructive experience that strengthens instead of weakens love.

Avoid the words "always" and "never." A person who's told "you're always late" or "you're never thoughtful" feels like a hopeless case for whom change is impossible.

Stick to the subject. If the disagreement is about overspending, don't introduce other issues.

Appreciate the other's right to a different point of view. At the moment it may not make sense, but when emotions cool you might see it differently.

Don't attack the other person's self-esteem. Pointing up past failures or a physical feature about which the other is sensitive is destructive and defeating to both partners.

Express feelings as calmly as possible. Hysteria and tears can be emotional blackmail.

Choose an appropriate time and place. A confrontation in front of others, or one begun the moment a person comes home, is off to a bad start.

Never turn to physical violence. Once unleashed, there's no telling where it will stop.

Know when to end a quarrel. Sometimes a fight needs to be ended before the disagreement is resolved. It's better to take up the matter at another time than to accept an unsatisfactory solution.

A constructive fight can be a sign that the relationship is alive and well. It says that two people care enough to take down the barriers or — better yet — never let them build up.

Good marriages develop; they are fashioned
out of long hours of doubt and despair
and adjustment and compromise.

Dorothy T. Samuel

Communicating
with
Love

Early in our relationship, we do a lot of talking and touching as we attempt to convey our feelings and thus get to know the other person better. We each see every situation from a slightly different perspective, so the better we're able to express ourselves, the more likely we are to establish an open and honest marriage.

Less than half of the communicating we do is verbal. Most of it is done through non-verbal body language. Our sighs and shrugs and postures and facial expressions often speak the truth more consistently and with less clutter than do our words. A kiss, a slammed door, and a smile are clear expressions of how we're feeling.

When communication is a trusting experience, it serves as a bridge over which we cross the unknown spaces between individuals. It involves us in listening as well as in revealing, so that both partners grow in knowledge of the other. In its most useful form, communication is talking *with,* not *at,* someone.

There are times when we'll have anger to communicate. Rather than lash out, we need to remind ourselves that an angry explosion may blow up the bridge between us and cause great pain. So rather than blow up, let's speak up—carefully and with purpose. Instead of a cruel attack, we can describe our feelings, admitting that "I feel so...." rather than accusing that "you make me feel so...." The honest admission of a deep feeling takes courage, but it is well worth the risk. Often, it will encourage our mate to reveal his or her feelings as well. In this way, we have a constructive encounter instead of a defensive or hostile scene. Although the bridge between us may shake a bit, it remains intact, making it possible to clarify and improve our relationship.

The best communication involves listening with love in both verbal and non-verbal situations so that we're open to receiving whatever the message may be. When listening with our heart, we'll often discover that what our mate needs the most at the moment is reassurance that she or he is an okay and an all right person. Then, a hug is the most necessary and loving action we can take, and there's no mistaking its meaning.

42

It is impossible to overemphasize the immense
need...to be really listened to, to be taken
seriously, to be understood.... No one can
develop freely in this world and find full
life without feeling understood by at least
one person.

Paul Tournier

Freeing the Sexual Self

Sex is an expression of love to be experienced and enjoyed, not merely an act to perform. It enlivens and enriches marriage, but since each of us has a different attitude toward sexual intimacy, it's likely to take a while before we find mutually satisfying ways of making love.

We begin freeing ourselves by believing that the words "dirty" and "normal" should not be applied to sex life. Our experiences should become as unique as our marriage and as meaningful as we're capable of making them. As our sense of warmth and security grows, so too does our ability to give and receive love.

Human sexuality is a sensual experience that involves not only physical love-making but all the ways we interact as male and female. Love-making is, however, the most personal way we have of expressing our feelings and is neither a duty nor a privilege of marriage. Rather, it is a gift that comes with life, and it is meant to be shared.

Being comfortable with our own sexuality is important. If we feel guilty about certain acts or have negative feelings that keep us from full participation, it helps to remember that these attitudes were learned. Likewise, a freer and healthier attitude can also be learned.

We gather information by reading manuals on sex, but knowledge alone isn't the answer. We also need to improve our emotional life as a couple. Since techniques without tenderness create no love, we turn to gentleness and kindness as stepping stones to sexual fulfillment.

Setting aside time for sex when we will be rested and alert increases our potential for satisfaction. Then, alone with our mate in an atmosphere of privacy, we have the opportunity to be free as lovers. Respect and trust enable us to shed our masks along with our clothes and to be real to one another.

In such a time of intimacy, neither of us knows for sure how the other feels until we share. That's the key to freedom in love-making. Sharing what we like and dislike—as well as what we're not sure of but think we might enjoy—and listening to our mate's suggestions lead to a willingness to make our sex life an adventure in love.

46

The good life exists, here on earth: it exists in the act of loving.

Joyce Carol Oates

Taking
Time
Alone

We marry with the idea of sharing our whole life with another person. In giving up our separateness, we anticipate being known in depth by another human being. Before long, however, we discover that, no matter how much in love we may be, we need time alone and so does our mate.

Although we recognize this need for solitude, it's easy to look at a crowded schedule and tell ourselves such luxury isn't possible. What we must first have is a strong conviction that being alone with our private thoughts and dreams nourishes the spirit and makes us a more loving, giving person. Then, we will create the time to be alone, knowing it's not a luxury but a necessity.

How will we find the time for solitude? Often, we have to steal it from our day in bits and pieces. Maybe it's a stroll on our lunch hour or a leisurely drive to the store. To fit time to be alone into our schedule in a more regular way takes a little planning. Getting up earlier than necessary gives us the opportunity to read, pray, meditate, or arrange a vase of flowers picked from the garden. One night a week can be reserved for such private interests as stamp collecting, ham radio, or records. One day of the weekend might be set aside to pursue such solitary interests as writing, sewing, or painting.

Each of us has different needs for closeness and distance. For some couples, it works well to be apart for a few days or even weeks at a time. Such an arrangement requires a basic trust in the relationship. When we truly love someone, we don't have to be with them physically to feel their presence. The thought of the other is a source of warmth and security that brings us together even over long distances.

Aloneness presents us with an opportunity to think creatively about our life and our marriage. It's a time to ask, "What am I becoming as a person?" and "What are we creating as a couple?" Solitude offers us a chance to refresh ourselves and thus develop a new outlook on any problems we might have in our marriage. Often, rejoining our mate leads to heightened intimacy, and when both mates find renewal through aloneness, the time that is shared becomes increasingly precious.

There are times when everyone craves privacy, especially because of the busy pace of our lives today. We should be entitled to time alone without guilt. Forcing two people to share every thought, every activity, every free moment together... is unnatural.

Paula and Dick McDonald

Growing
in
Intimacy

It's difficult to reveal ourselves totally and become intimate partners on the marital journey, but narrowing the emotional distance between partners is a beneficial goal. Doing so frees a couple to sense the full joy of living as husband and wife.

Intimacy is much more than togetherness. It is an inner feeling of warmth and closeness, an at-homeness we feel with our marriage partner, which develops over a period of time. To grow in such intimacy requires that we open ourselves directly, revealing our longings, hopes, fears, and dreams. Only in knowing can we understand, and only in understanding can we come to care deeply about our partner's well-being and growth as a person.

The rhythm of marriage includes cycles of moving toward and moving away from one another. No matter how great a degree of intimacy we may reach at any given time, it is not something we achieve once and for all. Rather, it changes with the seasons of marriage and must be nurtured throughout life.

It is best to remember, however, that each of us differs in our capacity for closeness. Some of us can relate in depth in certain areas of our lives and not in others. We might, for example, feel a sexual but not a spiritual intimacy or an emotional but not an intellectual intimacy. In every marriage there is untapped potential. Our experience of intimacy in one area suggests that such closeness can be achieved to a greater degree in other areas too.

To nurture intimacy, we must create time and space for being with our partner. As we settle into married life, it's easy to let careers, social commitments, sports, and causes consume our energy and deprive us of time we need to grow in awareness of one another. By saying "yes" when we can and "no" when we must to outside demands that become too great, we maintain a balance in our commitments that allows us to meet each other's deepest needs.

Growing in intimacy along the marital journey is to be always communicating our feelings and updating our dreams. It is to share celebrations in times of joy and hurts in times of pain. To do so is to dispel loneliness and know for ourselves the wonders that love can work.

The joy of marriage is hard to define, impossible
to promise. It can be lost if you let the possibility
of failure undermine your common sense
and defeat your determination or if you meet
the events of your marriage as obstacles
instead of opportunities.

Mary Williams

Looking beyond Ourselves

There is a yearning in all of us to find something we can believe in that will help us know peace of mind and heart in a troubled world. Even though we're married to a good and loving person whose affection is deeply satisfying, we still seek something more.

What is that something more? It's the spiritual dimension of life. It may appear as soft as a whisper that's easily ignored or as direct and distinct as a call urging us to work out a personal philosophy that will give meaning to the life and death experiences we all face.

Religions and philosophies suggest answers to life's mysteries, but essentially, no answers are satisfying until we have examined them and found them suitable for ourselves. However we deal with our spiritual dimension, the life philosophy we work out should not become a fixed state of mind. If it is to help us find meaning in difficult moments as well as in happier times, what we believe must change in order to meet our ever-increasing knowledge and awareness.

There is a special joy in marriage when two people share and are able to practice the same beliefs. But even if our beliefs and life philosophies differ widely from those of our partner, it's still possible to find a common core of meaning. In doing so, we have a very real hope of attaining spiritual intimacy.

Often, personal experiences take on a timeless quality. Time may literally stand still while we are making love, sharing a sunset, or serving the needs of another person for whom we have deep affection. The richness of music or meditation, or the experience of birth, may give us a sense of the spiritual and make us aware that we have shared in something beyond ourselves. At such a time we feel that we are indeed blessed by the fullness of life and of love.

By supporting and sustaining our partner in the quest to satisfy spiritual hunger, we can both hope to find the something more that gives us the peace we all are seeking.

In the wonder and ultimate mystery of love,
spiritual truths come alive; they take on
flesh-and-blood reality by being incarnated in
persons. Encountering the being of one's
partner — really seeing and experiencing that
unique person — is a deeply moving spiritual
meeting, spirit with spirit.

Howard J. Clinebell, Jr., and Charlotte H. Clinebell

Keeping Romance in Marriage

Romance is an emotional wonderland! It's a feeling that the stars are our stars, that the city is our city. It's an arm-in-arm walk in the rain, celebrating love that's as bright as fireworks. It's holding hands at a candlelight dinner and recalling the good times of ragtime or rock or reggae. It's a cherishing of what we've had with our mate and a dream of what we want.

Romance is impulsive. It's reflective. It's giggles and sighs. It's being lonely while the other is gone and then running to meet him or her with tears of joy.

The aura of romance under which two people discover their love for one another is a spontaneous and beautiful expression of what married life can be. But can we live forever in this emotional wonderland? Yes, it's possible. To do so, we have to realize that moments of ecstasy will—as our love matures—be spaced between periods that are less emotionally charged. In all marriages, there are everyday times of learning to live together successfully. There are times of adjustment and problem solving, times of loving and caring in quiet ways.

Even in the midst of these quieter times, however, romance still can be ours. In ways that are unique to us as a couple, we can make it clear that we're still the most important people in the world to each other.

Within marriage, the knowledge two people have of one another grows. And so does the possibility of thoughtfulness, which is at the heart of romance. The ways in which we can show our love and keep romance alive are virtually without limit. We might call just to say, "I love you!", give a gift when there's no special occasion, make love in the afternoon, or bring home flowers.

There will still be moments of ecstasy, of course, but for the most part, married people live in the midst of smaller joys. In sharing a rainbow arched across the sky or a cartoon that makes us smile, we are warmed by the presence of each other. Then, the realization comes that the romantic wonderland of our dating days was just a beginning. By working at making the most of marriage, we find romance flourishing and love growing deeper with time.

Love changes and grows....
The amount of love
generated in a good
marriage cannot be imagined
by the young couple
just starting out.

Dr. Joyce Brothers